Dubious Angels
poems after Paul Klee

2005

Dubious Angels

poems after Paul Klee

KEITH RATZLAFF

2005

Cover art: *Engel, übervoll,* by Paul Klee, 1939, 896 (WW 16)
(Angel, Brimful); watercolor and pencil on paper, mounted on cardboard;
52.5 x 36.5 cm; Zentrum Paul Klee, Bern, on loan from a private collection,
Ref. Nr. 8602
Author photo: Rhonda Patzia
Cover design, book design, and production: C. L. Knight
Typesetting: Jill Ihasz
Type: titles set in Goudy Sans Light; text set in Galliard

Library of Congress Cataloging-in-Publication Data
Dubious Angels: Poems after Paul Klee by Keith Ratzlaff — First Edition
ISBN 0938078-83-6 (paper)
ISBN 0938078-85-2 (cloth)
Library of Congress Control Number: 2005900048

This publication is sponsored in part by a grant
from the Florida Department of State,
Division of Cultural Affairs, and the Florida Arts Council.

Anhinga Press Inc. is a nonprofit corporation dedicated wholly
to the publication and appreciation of fine poetry.

For personal orders, catalogs and information write to:
Anhinga Press
P.O. Box 10595
Tallahassee, Florida 32302
Web site: www.anhinga.org
E-mail: info@anhinga.org

Published in the United States
by Anhinga Press
Tallahassee, Florida
First Edition, 2005

CONTENTS

ACKNOWLEDGMENTS

The Common Review: "Unfinished Angel"

Denver Quarterly: "In the Waiting Room of Angelhood"
(as "Fitful Angel")

The Colorado Review: "Angelus Dubiosus"

The Journal: "Angel Applicant," "Angel in Kindergarten,"
"Approximate Angel," "Forgetful Angel"

Tampa Review: "Angel in Kindergarten," "Angelus Militans,"
"Vermin Angel," "Vigilant Angel"

"Angel Applicant," "Forgetful Angel," "Angel in the Making"
(as "Gladiolus") and "In the Waiting Room of Angelhood"
(as "Fitful Angel") also appear in *Man Under A Pear Tree,*
Anhinga Press, 1997.

Thanks to my Central College colleagues (too many to
mention) who let me badger them with questions about art,
music, philosophy and religion — but special thanks to Dr.
Silvia Rode for her help with translating Klee's titles. I'm
indebted to the Ragdale Foundation and the Millay Colony for
space and time to complete these poems. As always, my literary
brothers Jeff Gundy, Clint McCown, Kevin Stein and Dean
Young were the best readers any writer could have. This book is
for Treva, who is an angel (and reader) in her own right.

PREFACE

In the 18 months before his death in June 1940, Paul Klee painted and drew almost 1,500 images, 50 or so of them angels. It was an amazing creative burst made even more so by the fact he was dying of schleroderma, a painful drying up of the body's connective tissues that had curtailed not only his painting but his cooking (he was a gourmet) and his music (he was a nearly professional-level violinist). Winged figures had appeared before in Klee's work, but these late angels are obviously different — cruder in a way, but also funny, irreverent, poignant figures caught somehow between earth and heaven. I wouldn't be the first to say that they are stand-ins for Klee himself. And the angels do have the feel of personal tragedy. Not only had Klee's health been broken, but the Nazis had run him out of Germany and ruined his teaching career; they'd ridiculed his work in the Degenerate Art exhibitions. Klee had, in fact, been reading and re-reading the *Orestia* in the months before his death. But if the events surrounding the angels seem tragic, their technique is vintage Klee: ironic, playful, serious and comic, a culmination of what he had practiced and taught for 25 years. He was one of the first great teachers of what we've come to call "the process" — taking line (and color) "on a walk" as he told his students.

I don't mean for these poems to speak for Paul Klee, nor have I wanted to turn the drawings into illustrations for the poems, or to make the poems into passive ekphrastic exercises; they aren't written to identify with Klee's sense of his own mortality (I am not dying in any ways but the ordinary ones). What I hope I've done is approximated Klee's tragicomic voice and his jazz-like technique with my own, and given the angels voices that do justice to the bodies Paul Klee created for them.

ILLUSTRATIONS

All illustrations are by Paul Klee (1879 - 1940).

PLATE 1 (page 4)
vergesslicher Engel, 1939, 880 (VV 20) *(Forgetful Angel)*
Pencil on paper, mounted on cardboard
29.5 x 21 cm; Zentrum Paul Klee, Bern, Inv. Nr. Z 1899, Ref. Nr. 8586

PLATE 2 (page 6)
Engel im Kindergarten, 1939, 968 (AB 8) *(Angel in Kindergarten)*
Pencil on paper, mounted on cardboard
29.5 x 21 cm; Zentrum Paul Klee, Bern, Inv. Nr. Z 1939, Ref. Nr. 8674

PLATE 3 (page 8)
letzter Erdenschritt, 1939, 893 (WW 13) *(Last Earthly Step)*
Pencil on paper, mounted on cardboard
29.5 x 21 cm; Zentrum Paul Klee, Bern, Inv. Nr. Z 1909, Ref. Nr. 8599

PLATE 4 (page 13)
Engel im Werden, 1934, 204 (U 4) *(Angel in the Making)*
Oil on primed canvas, mounted on plywood
51 x 51 cm; Zentrum Paul Klee, on loan from a private collection,
Ref. Nr. 6742

PLATE 5 (page 14)
Engel-Anwärter, 1939, 856 (UU16) *(Angel Applicant)*
Gouache, black ink, and pencil on wove paper mounted on light cardboard
48.9 x 34 cm; The Metropolitan Museum of Art, The Berggruen Klee
Collection, 1984. (1984.315.60) Photograph ©1985 The Metropolitan
Museum of Art

PLATE 6 (page 18)
Getier, 1939, 960 (ZZ 20) *(Creature)*
Pencil on paper, mounted on cardboard
27 x 17.8 cm; Zentrum Paul Klee, Bern, Inv. Nr. Z 1931, Ref. Nr. 8666

PLATE 7 (page 20)
Angelus militans, 1939, 1028 (DE 8) *(Angelus militans)*
Crayon on paper, mounted on cardboard
44.3 x 29.9 cm; Zentrum Paul Klee, Bern, Inv. Nr. Z 1976, Ref. Nr. 8734

PLATE 8 (page 24)
engelsam, 1939, 593 (EE 13) *(Angel-like)*
Pencil on paper, mounted on cardboard
29.7 x 20.9 cm; Zentrum Paul Klee, Bern, Inv. Nr. Z 1726, Ref. Nr. 8299

PLATE 9 (page 26)
altkluger Engel, 1939, 873 (VV 13) *(Precocious Angel)*
Pencil on paper, mounted on cardboard
29.5 x 21 cm; Zentrum Paul Klee, Bern, Inv. Nr. Z 1893, Ref. Nr. 8579

PLATE 10 (page 29)
armer Engel, 1939, 854 (UU 14) *(Poor Angel)*
Watercolor and tempera on primed paper, mounted on cardboard
48.6 x 32.5 cm; Zentrum Paul Klee, Bern, on loan from a private collection,
Ref. Nr. 8560

PLATE 11 (page 30)
Engel, noch tastend, 1939, 1193 (MN 13) *(Angel, Still Groping)*
Crayon, colored paste and watercolor on paper, mounted on cardboard
29.4 x 20.8 cm; Zentrum Paul Klee, Bern, on loan from a private collection,
Ref. Nr. 8900

PLATE 12 (page 34)
es weint, 1939, 959 (ZZ 19) *(It weeps)*
Pencil on paper, mounted on cardboard
29.5 x 21 cm; Zentrum Paul Klee, Bern, Inv. Nr. Z 1930, Ref. Nr. 8665

PLATE 13 (page 38)
Engel des alten Testamentes, 1939, 875 (VV 15) *(Angel of the Old Testament)*
Pencil on paper, mounted on cardboard
29.5 x 21 cm; Zentrum Paul Klee, Bern, Inv. Nr. Z 1895, Ref. Nr. 8581

PLATE 14 (page 40)
Engel im Boot, 1939, 881 (WW 1) *(Angel in the Boat)*
Pencil on paper, mounted on cardboard
29.5 x 21 cm; Zentrum Paul Klee, Bern, Inv. Nr. Z 1900, Ref. Nr. 8587

PLATE 15 (page 44)
hässlicher Engel, 1939, 1102 (Hi 2) *(Ugly Angel)*
Crayon on paper, mounted on cardboard
29.5 x 20.8 cm: Zentrum Paul Klee, Bern, Inv. Nr. Z 2008, Ref. Nr. 8808

PLATE 16 (page 46)
unfertiger Engel, 1939, 841 (UU 1) *(Unfinished Angel)*
Pencil on paper, mounted on cardboard
29.5 x 21 cm; Zentrum Paul Klee, Bern, Inv. Nr. Z 1881, Ref. Nr. 8547

PLATE 17 (page 48)
Osaña, 1939, 883 (WW 3) *(Hosanna)*
Pencil on paper, mounted on cardboard
29.5 x 21 cm; Zentrum Paul Klee, Bern, Inv. Nr. Z 1902, Ref. Nr. 8589

PLATE 18 (page 51)
Engel, noch weiblich, 1939, 1016 (CD 16) *(Angel, Still Female)*
Crayon over paste on paper, mounted on cardboard
41.7 x 29.4 cm; Zentrum Paul Klee, Bern, Inv. Nr. F 135, Ref. Nr. 8722

PLATE 19 (page 52)
wachsamer Engel, 1939, 859 (UU 19) *(Vigilant Angel)*
Pen and tempera on primed newsprint, mounted on cardboard
48.5 x 33 cm; Zentrum Paul Klee, on loan from a private collection,
Ref. Nr. 8565

PLATE 20 (page 56)
ein alter Musiker tut engelhaft, 1939, 888 (WW 8)
(An Old Musician Acts Angel-like)
Pencil on paper, mounted on cardboard
29.5 x 21 cm; Zentrum Paul Klee, Bern, Inv. Nr. Z 1905, Ref. Nr. 8594

PLATE 21 (page 60)
anderer Engel vom Kreuz, 1939, 1026 (DE 6) *(Other Angel of the Cross)*
Crayon on paper, mounted on cardboard
45.6 x 30.3 cm; Zentrum Paul Klee, Bern, Inv. Nr. Z 1974, Ref. Nr. 8732

PLATE 22 (page 62)
Zweifelnder Engel, 1940, 341 (F 1) *(Doubting Angel)*
Pastel on paper, mounted on folded cardboard
29.7 x 20.9 cm; Zentrum Paul Klee, Bern, Inv. Nr. Z 2236, Ref. Nr. 9360

PLATE 23 (page 64)
im Vorzimmer der Engelschaft, 1939, 845 (UU 5)
(In the Antechamber of Angelhood)
Pencil on paper, mounted on cardboard
29.5 x 21 cm; Zentrum Paul Klee, Bern, Inv. Nr. Z 1883, Ref. Nr. 8551

PLATE 24 (page 66)
mehr Vogel, 1939, 939 (YY 19) *(More Bird)*
Pencil on paper, mounted on cardboard
21 x 29.5 cm; Zentrum Paul Klee, Bern, Inv. Nr. Z 1914, Ref. Nr. 8645

PLATE 25 (page 71)
Engel, übervoll, 1939, 896 (WW 16) *(Angel, Brimful)*
Watercolor and pencil on paper, mounted on cardboard
52.5 x 36.5 cm; Zentrum Paul Klee, Bern, on loan from a private collection,
Ref. Nr. 8602

PLATE 26 (page 72)
angelus dubiosus, 1939, 930 (YY 10) *(Angelus Dubiosus)*
Watercolor on paper, mounted on cardboard
29.5 x 21 cm; Zentrum Paul Klee, Bern, on loan from a private collection,
Ref. Nr. 8636

PLATE 27 (page 78)
Engel voller hoffnung, 1939, 892 (WW 12) *(Angel Full of Hope)*
Pencil on paper, mounted on cardboard
29.5 x 21 cm; Zentrum Paul Klee, Bern, Inv. Nr. Z 1908, Ref. Nr. 8598

Man is half prisoner, half borne on wings.
— Paul Klee, *The Thinking Eye*

Dubious Angels

FORGETFUL ANGEL

Memory is a minimal condition.
— Kirkegaard

Here I lose
my own hands
even in my own lap

But that's not the point

Here everything
is performance
which is heaven's great secret

Now and now

Memory is not minimum
but minimal
not little, but least

Like a mask but thinner

Like the moon — whose motion
isn't memory
but the act of being the moon

I've forgotten how to say this

I remember rain
I miss
the way it wandered

1939 vv 20 Vergeslicher Engel

PLATE 1

through the entire
afternoon
The way the world settled

The cat's red dish
the rain
gradually filling it

Action and not plot

God is a chair
to sit in
and the act of sitting

It makes all the difference

And yet rain, how it was
like something
here and not here

Like a ring once on my finger
Like a road
disappearing in the trees

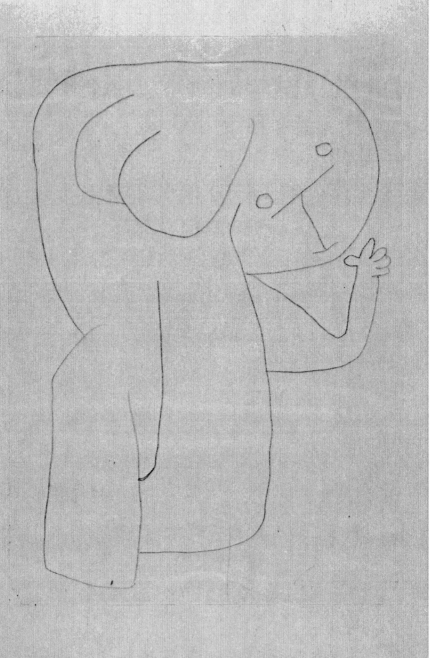

1939 A58   Engel im Kindergarten

PLATE 2

ANGEL IN KINDERGARTEN

We went on a field trip
to the garden of saws,
that place of blades and dirt,
pink shoots of kerf and sharpness
where I thought if I raised my hand
even the air there would slice it.
How would I ever learn to run
like God with knives in his pockets,
pins in his mouth?

I'm learning to keep to myself,
keep my hands at home —
those small things yellow and blue
you wouldn't notice with all
the other things I have on my mind.
I keep them hidden like mirrors
in my pockets, like numbers:
one then another. One thumbnail
is the only sharp thing
I'm trusted with, so
I hold it in my mouth.
In the garden of birds
I asked for wings — two of them —
so I could begin to count my
way into the air — but instead
God gave me buttocks.
Which is a start.
This is the only joke I know.

1939 W.13   Letzter Erdenschritt

PLATE 3

LAST EARTHLY STEP

For a man walking is a shifting of weights
And when a man faints he falls off his chair
And when he falls he becomes disguised as a block of stone
For we are a dream of instability
For we are a drama of horizontals
How we last and are last
How our hair goes disguised as a shroud in the little wind

For the mailman walking is an orphan
Or in the Old High German, a migrant
Step after anonymous step between house after anonymous
    house
Or in the Old Church Slavonic, *rabu,* a robot,
    a thing so desperately free it has no choice
For the word "last" is a meditation on stopping and continuing
Like a dying man making plans
Last word, last rites, last hurrah, last minute
And intensity is of no avail
And memory is of no avail
How we are a dream of lying down
Like a dying man in a boat planning a haircut
Last gasp
And then you become the word "falling"

(When I was little I wanted to grow up to be the word
    "pendulum," that sad, half circle winding gradually down,
    but each swing its own swing, each step its own step
    between unrelated houses in the endless suburbs)
And perspective is of no avail, is only a trick of the intellect, an
    illusion of foreground and background
Fall short, fall back, fall for, fall flat
Fall out, fall from grace, fall guy, falling star

For there is no angel of history
And there is no storm called progress
Only the single catastrophe of this moment
Last supper, last straw, last laugh
Then clouds for the last time

ANGEL IN THE MAKING

There has never been a shortage
of places the body wanted not
to be: in the lifeboat,
at the awards dinner, under the tree
after falling, in the tree hanging,
in the box, in the box exhumed.

Or here in a photo on an inside page
of the *New York Times:* a skeleton
from the African Burial Ground, hands
folded across the now-collapsed chest.
A gesture, the *Times* says, meant
to help the spirit find Africa

again. And now scaphoid,
the wrist's bone boat, rides
in what was the heart's little harbor.
And cuneiform the wrist's wedge,
and semilunar the wrist's half moon
rises over the ocean. Remember

how often the torso was just bloody
cloth, the groin a red triangle,
the arms fired and set adrift.
That's over. Now fingers, wrist,
ribs, spine are mixed, all crossed,
all merely cups in the same cupboard.

But spirit you were right all along —
the journey is a map of the body.
Here in the backwash of the chest,
above the Inlet of the Pelvis,
north of the great and nameless
Os Innominatum, here at the sternum

you crossed your two lucky arms
at the middle bone called Gladiolus —
north of Ensiform, the false one,
south of the Manubrium — Gladiolus,
also called the sword of the body,
once called the wild iris of Africa.

PLATE 4

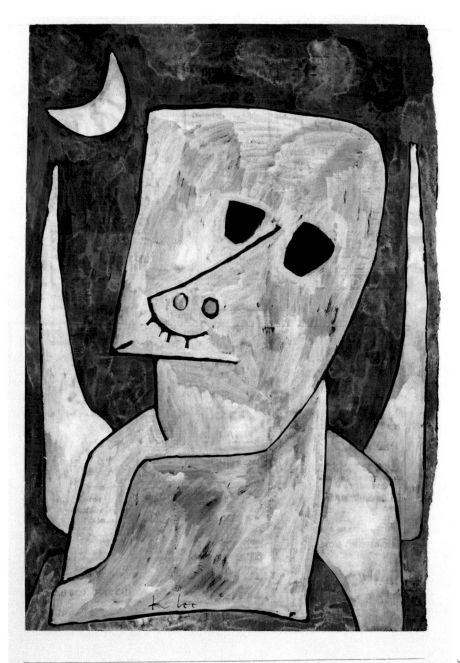

angegriffener Engel-Anwärter

PLATE 5

ANGEL APPLICANT

Because Paul Klee has stopped playing the violin
I am lifting my arms to heaven
Because in Switzerland you are nothing without wings
I am applying in place of Paul Klee, who lives in Switzerland
Once I applied in place of Mondrian
Because three is two put in motion
Because it is harder to apply in place of myself
Because obviously I was turned down
Once I applied as a man hanged in a barn behind a house Cezanne
    painted in Auvers
I am not immortal enough
If I were given the chance to remake the world I would defer
If I were on a third floor balcony I would test the railings
The barn behind the house with the blue door
I am not sure photography is an art
Because Klee has stopped cooking, too
Where else would I go
From the hayloft there was a grand view of the green Provence hills
The dry rope and the dry esophagus
Above my head starlings were in the rafters
There was the moon
I do not think irony has a place here
Van Gogh painted the same house — but not with such fervor
Because not everything is up to me
Not like Cezanne
Who signed his paintings with a little gallows for years he was
    so pleased
The rope and the twisted nature of the cedar
Pisarro and Cezanne in the clear Provence air
Their pallettes slowly brightening
Because he cannot swallow solid food
Red for Pisarro, Blue for Cezanne

Because Klee has given me three arms to raise
Because I will have to apply next as a woman in a late Picasso
     etching
And nobody wants that
Three arms
The moon above me
I had always been told birds living in your eaves were a sign of
     good luck
But I don't know why

Because in the Talmud, a man turns into a worm but I am not in
     the Talmud
Where I am the ground is mottled; the room is small and the flat
     has sheets hanging in the hallway
And my legs are vague
And because the moon
Who dies in photographs? At what moment?
If I thought there was a chance
Because the moon
Is pulling my head up into the first prong of a crown

VERMIN ANGEL

From now on, all worms,
all words turn.
Heaven has become a republic.

Without the mole's low
vertigo,
without weasels,

without the ferret's
rhapsodic
vertebrae, or spiders

in the briars, the old
ribald tumult
of a snake in the pants —

all you have is Arcadia
in a wig,
a makeshift resort of clean claws.

Without gobshites
and schisms,
the tapeworm's sinister *volta*,

without rat the vermin
attorney —
you wouldn't know paradise

if it bit you. God knows
staying true
to your own nature

1939 ZZ20 Getier

PLATE 6

is no great talent —
oversold,
rectal, contrite.

But to know your own seams
and sutures,
your own peevish wrangles,

the truant
you are
from nares to sphincter

is something we were
born again to
and again. Even

our tongues in your armpit
praise God.
Even our teeth will have wings.

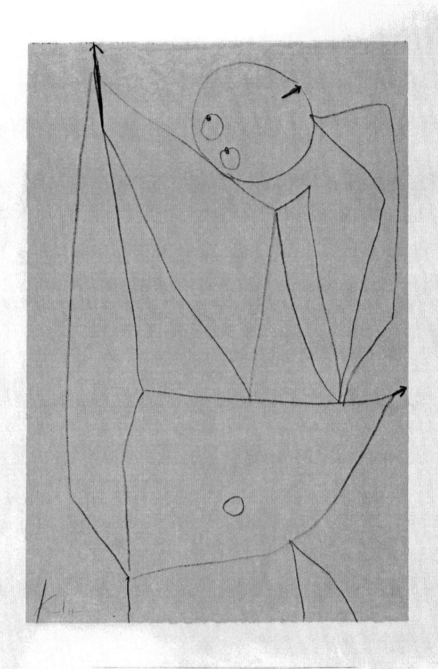

1939 DE1 Angelus militans

PLATE 7

ANGELUS MILITANS

The question of life and death rests with the small arrow.
— Paul Klee, *Pedagogical Sketchbook*

When we first shot our pistols
in the air,
we were innocents. New Year's Eve

and we brought down a snow shower.
So next we fired
warning shots, and our own bullets

rained down in the fountain,
pinged on our heads.
God had turned gravity on us

like a weapon, and that started that.
At first we marched
and sang knife songs, did and undid

our epaulettes, blazed at the stars
until we could see
them burning. But then we stood

on one foot to make ourselves lighter,
dug wells in ourselves
in order to be lighter, pushed

our heads into the air as if
we could turn them
into the balloons which they became.

And we sharpened our tongues and
threw down our pants,
and thought we should cut off our pricks

to make ourselves lighter, but pricks
know which way is up.
And besides, we are not crazy like that.

We will save what can be saved.
It is a question
of life and death. We will be

arrows but lighter than arrows —
the teeth of dogs,
the corners of tables, the taper

of javelins, the memories of tusks,
the shadow of jets
and the buildings they fly into.

We have outlawed the spiral
because it is always
of two minds. We have abolished

trajectory because it cannot be true,
the center of the earth
because it leads to falling.

Circles, those pacifists, we have given
the chance to join us,
be our eyes (even though we would

yank them out to make ourselves lighter),
tied their hands,
marched them out like infantry

to show God their whites. And then
there will be arrows.
Everyone's. And then we shall see.

APPROXIMATE ANGEL

I was almost no good
as a prize fighter.
I was fast — my feet almost
hovered above the mat —
but my gloves were loaded
only with horseshoes of air,
and the mugs I boxed said
it was like being roundhoused
with paper streamers,
or cauliflower florets,
or flowers in general —
and then I was down
on something like my ass
or my luck. Heaven
is an exact sort of place,
and I have only something
resembling a left jab.

It was all Marquis of Queensberry,
all joke and no punch line:
Rule 4. If either man fall through weakness or otherwise,
   he must get up unassisted;
Rule 5. A man hanging on the ropes in a helpless state,
   with his toes off the ground, shall be considered down;
Rule 11. No shoes or boots with springs allowed.

I mean, what else did I have?
I mean, it was all Duke of York
who put the duke in put up yours,
but that's a joke, too,
Cockney slang: York
rhymes with fork

1939 EE 13   Engelsam

PLATE 8

out of fingers out of fist, oh
never mind. You can see why
I'll have to fight my way in,
head low, guard up
like something not myself,
planting blow after hook after haymaker
right on God's kisser.

1939 v v 13 althluger Engel

PLATE 9

PRECOCIOUS ANGEL

from the diaries of Paul Klee

I didn't believe in God; other little boys were always saying,
parrot-like, that God was constantly watching us. I was
persuaded of the inferior nature of such a belief. One day
a very old grandmother died in our barrack-like apartment
house. The little boys claimed that she was now an angel;
I wasn't in the least convinced.

Often I said I served Beauty by drawing her enemies.

I planned a poem with the following line-endings:
Eyes/breast/desire/night/laughed/sleep/met/
companion/order/trees/dream/night of the heart.

When I was ten I went to the opera for the first time. They
were playing *Il Trovatore*, and I was struck by the fact that
these people suffered so much and that they were never calm
and seldom gay. But I quickly felt at home in the pathetic
style. I began to like the raving Leonora, and when her hands
fumbled wildly about her mouth, I thought I recognized in
this gesture a desperate grab at her denture; I even saw the
glitter of a few out flung teeth. In the Bible people used to
rend their garments: why shouldn't pulling out your teeth be
a beautiful and moving expression of despair?

POOR ANGEL

Again the sun
is in its blue box,
that square of everything
we call the sky,
and the river outside town
we call the Des Moines —
even though "Des Moines"
doesn't mean anything
in French or English but might,
one anthropologist says,
mean "shitfaces"
in a forgotten Indian dialect.
And this mutter of everything
is called where we live,
and the frost-bitten garden
is my garden. The marigolds
hanging their heads
are called what happens.

And my pocket is the place
for a pocket,
and this square of ground
is a place for a chair,
and when I sit here
I am called the poor master
of the frazzled garden,
a minor painter
in a small workshop.
When I lift my head
it's to prove I'm not
a marigold.

1939 W14   xxxx Engel

PLATE 10

1939 \ N 13 Engel noch tastend

PLATE II

ANGEL, STILL GROPING

It was the day we couldn't coax the cat from under
    the house next door
Blue Jay in the maple, his italicized crest
The day we thought of cutting off our right pinkies and mailing
    them to the president
Like an exclamation, something being underlined
Vallejo says one wing can't be a wing, but he meant the day
    is an orphan
And it's that same day's red salt in my mouth
The same birds assembling on the lawn
The same day of authorities by the gate
The same body — I almost said boy when I don't even know —
    they found at the scene
Which is what made it a scene to begin with
The day the microphones showed up to make a scene
The day the duke showed up to make a scene
    black beads around my neck, Florentine sleeves,
    burgundy under green velvet, the ermine in my lap
The paper said, "A friend was trying to resuscitate when
    the authorities arrived"
Somebody heard someone yelling something that night
And the yellow tape that made a scene
The day a crime scene with birds attached
And scooters with kids attached
And why not one wing?
Why not be an angel if someone calls you one?
The power was out on the north side that night
She said, "I heard someone hollering wake up, wake up"
He said, "But to have someone come out here, and kill someone
    in the drive, that's not good"
The duke coming through the door

The police picking through the yard like birds
The day the cat brought the pigeon in the house and hid
 behind the stove
The day North Koreans rushed a diplomatic compound
 in Beijing
The pigeon lay absolutely still
How it let the cat strip the skin off its neck
The scene I made, hitting the cat with the broom, yelling
 because I am always the pigeon in this story
Until our hands were stumps
Mailing finger after finger to the president
To the Air Force Command's third wing
I swept the pigeon into the dust pan with the broom
And the day full of exhaust as usual
The duke coming through the door as usual
My arms in the air as usual
One of them
Someone was hollering wake up, wake up
The pigeon, the usual dust
I meant to dump the body in the trash and it was noon
On the news the Pope in a green robe crouched behind a lectern
And then the mystery: the pigeon stirs and flaps, gains a little
 altitude, then flies away around the corner of the house
Followed by the cat
Who thinks his collar is a medal for valor, for storming
 the ammo dump
The cat who was later hit by a truck and lived, but wouldn't
 come out from under the neighbor's house for days
The plan was thousands of us, to the president, we'd know each
 other on the street like Masons

And if the whole sky were one blue wing what then
The orphan wing of the day, the unborn wing of the night
The duke coming through the door, stage left
My eyes raised then lowered like the moon
My sleeves slashed
In a green robe he no longer had the body to fill
Whoever knows the answer should raise his hand
The birds are looking the wrong direction
And here's the real moon, a little smear, its head bowed
The birds, like us, on the run
Give them this message

1939 33/19   es weint

PLATE 12

CRYING ANGEL

Nothing prepared me for heaven.
Its scaffolds — street after street —
halls leading to halls,
rooms papered with distance

as if heaven were only perspective,
a vanishing point drawing us
until we vanished. And if
I am crying, it's for small things:

staplers, bowls, gloves, spoons
on their pedestals, their ideal forms
lost at the ends of corridors —
for Music in its winged box,

Math's fulcrum and see-saw,
Geography's colored pins, its there, there.

How did we ever come to think
the single world was precious,
the model for us to love —
one town, one house, one sky,

one woman, the mole on her back —
when it is the universe, its gaps,
the mileage between its outposts,
God loves and is his image?

They weren't lies after all, the stories
where we are transmuted into stars

or into water lost in the infinity
of itself. Who could have imagined

God's need for distance,
his hurling us away to be near him?

ANGEL OF THE OLD TESTAMENT

Remember the day after
the day in the canoe,
your arms wrangling about
which of them hurt more?
That lovely symmetry of ache
when you had two of everything —
arms, lips, minds, nostrils,
profiles, nipples, eyes?

Remember the crooked moon,
its imitation of a one-eyed man?
Red vines climbing over the house
like vengeance? Remember the kid
who shot out his eye with a BB gun?
He's turned TV preacher,
eye-patched and piratical,
who pounds the podium
and saith (now)
he plucked out that eye himself
because it hath so offended God.
The holiest of acts is always
to turn on ourselves.
Like those dogs, like the dentist
who pulled his own teeth,
like those starlings
trapped in the attic until
nine bodies and only seven heads.

Remember those rooms
we found after the war,
with profiles burned
into the walls to prove

1939 Engel des alten Testamentes

PLATE 13

all we leave is a summary?
Like the new moon
burned into the sky
again and again,
the same kind of darkness?

1939 W.14   Engel im Boot

PLATE 14

ANGEL IN A BOAT

In a troubled sea, once,
I prayed dear gods
save me; and they did
but sank my boat.
They are so literal.
Once across the street
a window flared yellow
then out, and I imagined
a ship in trouble
but what did I know
then, about trouble?

And now we are mutinied,
the crew flinging themselves
overboard, as if the body
were its own bad luck
and could be saved by drowning.
We are fire in the hold,
windows flaring, the boat
sawing at the waves
and the sea sawing back
like double magicians
racing through the act.

Dear gods again,
you who are stalwart and useless
as stones in our shoes,
whatever you do with this prayer
remember once even you
in your chairs were troubled
by the sea, at its rooms,
its beds too large, too soft,

how much of it was and was
not you. Remember when
the sun flared on a window
and someone — God himself? —
raised his hands in anger
and your hearts were banging
on the cabin door to be
oh please oh please
let out? How he lowered
his arms, unbent himself,
leaned and kissed your hair?

UGLY ANGEL

It is in the center that our bodies betray us.
— Paul Klee, *The Thinking Eye*

Because the day I tried on
symmetry
my heart ran away.

Because beauty isn't
in the balance
of the tightrope walker

but in his wavering; not in
the upright jug
but in the jug tipped and poured.

Our bodies betray us
down the center:
two eyes, one sex,

two nostrils, one mouth,
the violin's
shape but not its music.

Because Manet's *Olympia*
lies on the divan,
legs crossed, her hand

like a spider — a flower —
on her thigh,
a camellia off center in her hair.

1939 Hi2 hässlicher Engel

PLATE 15

And what would I do
with my heart
if it ever came back?

How would I keep it in line?
Its red and blue
engines, its off-kilter demands?

Because the trillium —
called Birthroot,
called Wake-robin —

is blooming red now
in the May woods.
And I've picked one

like a three-lobed heart,
and pinned it
dead center in my hair

to keep it from sliding
terrifyingly
over my left ear.

1939 UII 1   unfertiger Engel

PLATE 16

UNFINISHED ANGEL

I was a student once in Macy's autumn finishing school for
young women. I had the edges of a rock, a pine cone. It was
impossible: the book lost its balance again and again on my
head; the Birds of Paradise squawked in the centerpieces;
I could not seem to cross my legs correctly at the ankle.

There were the misshapen ball gowns we had no breasts to hold
up. There were the black lunches with our mothers. There were
the traffic patterns of the dinner party charted on calm, gridded
paper — when what I loved were the collisions of dishes, trains
off the tracks, explosions at intersections, ambulances. Wherever
I was going, Macy's let me go without one polite word to say.

Dear God, I am all barb, all rachis, quill and vane, all stinger
and burr, all hem come undone. When Macy's gives up on you,
all that's left is thee, or thou who are, or am, or art in heaven,
ballyhooed be thy name. Thy kingdom comely as the earth we
thought was heaven. Lead us to, if not temptation, that place
where we will be rough enough for mercy. For thine is the
kingdom and the power and the story of the wind-like grace
that grinds us down and up, world without amen.

1939 W3   Osana

OSAÑA (SAINT OF MANTUA)

I fall for God each time
like a schoolgirl, like a sparrow.
One minute I'm in the kitchen
the next I'm on my knees
in the garden yelling my name.
Hosanna. I never know
whether I'm asking for help
or giving it. I never know
which wing will unfold,
which stigmata in my hand will open
and who is hysterical then?
Hosanna. Ecstasy
is a kind of rapture, a kind
of doubt, a kind of Tourette's,
a kind of trance, a kind of terror
I took the veil to have. Hosanna
the tigers of the spirit. Hosanna
the interjection of my name
I would be delivered from —
but would also have tattooed
on my heart next to
the name of God which is,
of course, unspellable.
Hosanna rider and horse.
Hosanna the broken heart
and the cross springing from it.
Hosanna the way I take God
always back, the way I crawl
there each time in the lilies
hands tied, heart slung a little
lower in my chest — Hosanna —
kneeling and trembling.

ANGEL, STILL FEMALE

I thought we would leave behind
all dross, and the imprints of dross:
shadows, television, the X-rays of my chest,
that picture on my mother's piano
of that day in the snow with the dog.

(Sparrows used to hang in my winter maple
like clothespins I'd forgotten.)

I thought somehow we turned
into light, but it turns out
we are only sparrows,
or pictures of sparrows,
just the same dogs leashed
to same the garage, with the same breasts,
the same red between our legs
and dangling from our mouths,
the same animals we ever were.

(And sparrows fall, the Bible says,
because they have such talent for falling,
and we have such need to be taught,
and God such wonder that he watches.)

It turns out I am still that girl
in the photograph, in that moment,
in the forever time of the golden dog
cut loose and running rings around me.
That dog in the snow so happy he was a blur.

- 39 ZО 16 - Engel, noch weiblich

PLATE 18

PLATE 19

VIGILANT ANGEL

with apologies to the New York Times

Because of an editing error, an article in The Arts on Tuesday
    misstated the location of the American Bible Society.
The film was "Funny Girl" not "Hello Dolly."
It is 3 not 2; 70 percent, not 80; they are not currently serving
    on that board; it was 1987 not 1992.
They are not testing the organ donor's brain for such evidence.
The spokesman now says he was mistaken and the conversation
    never occurred.
The article also misstated the admission policy of New York
    City museums for Sept. 11.
The society is at Broadway and 61st street, not 65th.
At least one, the Metropolitan, will charge its usual fees.
In Philip Glass's opera "Galileo Galilei," the progress of balls
    rolling downhill past unevenly spaced dividing lines was
    measured on a single inclined plane, not on different planes.
There may be more.
Not all will be free.
This will go on all day.
No one will actually
be eating children.
We apologize. Bells
will ring.

An article in Business Day misstated the ratio of the company's
    debt to its cash flow.
A front-page article misstated the estimate of people killed by
    war in Chechnya since 1994. Officials and human rights
    groups put it at 40,000 to 160,000 — not as high as
    200,000.
White lines will form on a black background.

It said the corporate world was sometimes less forgiving than
the political one.
It is between 5.9 and 6.3, not about 7.
Nothing could be further from the truth.
It did not rise 56.1 percent.
Someone's eyes will be peeled.
Someone's ear will turn to cauliflower.
The Arts Abroad column was simply a mess.
Elevators will descend.
We will have to be resigned.

Ms. Bryant was a former contestant, but not a former Miss
America.
The Famous Artists School in Wilton, Conn. has not closed.
She is Janet Napolitano, not Jane.
147 acres not 83.
He is Ron Wood, not Woods; the two are Billy Eckstine, not
Eckstein, and Ritchie Valens, not Richie; it is the Strokes,
not the Stokes.
It is at noon.
He is Benjamin Errett, not Everett.
She is Barbra, not Barbara.
Eugene Richardson, not Smith.
The three should have been invited to comment.
He said, "I wouldn't say that there is a fundamental
disagreement" between them.
Naftalis, not Neftalis.
Yolande not Yolanda.
Wenger, not Wagner.
Kim Suk Soo, not Kim Kuk Soo.

It was the Associated Press, not the Boston Globe.

A theater review of the 1933 play "Three-Cornered Moon"
cited "The Front Page" incorrectly among other snappy,
loopy and frenetic works that it predated.

The Irish music festival is spelled Fleadh Cheoil no hEireann.

Really.

The chairman's surname was misspelled. He is Labhras O Murchu,
not Murch.

The close is tomorrow night, not tonight.

It did not open yesterday.

A film review in Weekend about "All My Loved Ones," the story
of five brothers in Prague just before World War I
misidentifies the instrument played by the one who is not a
concert musician.

Omitted articles are online.

Write to Production Quality Control or telephone.

The Irish drum is a bodhran, not bodhrn.

We have misstated the size of Glen Ding.

Include a Postal Address.

Despite Schubert's lyric gift, he never achieved any particular
distinction in opera.

We apologize.

It is the violin, not the piano.

1939 N.8   ein alter Musiker tut engelhaft

PLATE 20

AN OLD MUSICIAN ACTS ANGELIC

And here's the old man
who thinks he's more angel than old,
more God than the orchestra.
It's such a small blasphemy,
pochettino, let it go. Let him
walk to the podium *andante*,
like a great guest conductor —
even though he's only won
a raffle to be here,
even though luck is only
one doppelgänger of grace.
It doesn't matter,
the orchestra knows what to do
and they are tender with him,
tenerezza, con tenerezza.
And no one knows which came first,
the fiddle or the fiddlehead fern,
the girl or the all-girl band,
but they take it *da capo*,
from the beginning. And
from his frantic, left-handed downbeat
blooms the first great chord
of the theme from *Star Wars*.
Please forgive the musical director,
we need new audiences, he thinks,
we need to start somewhere —
and it's such a small and terrible
mistake when there is Mendelssohn —
but let it go, *lacrimosa*, let it go,
since musicians are such minor
conduits of beauty, and
the violin is just an odd baby

tucked under our chins.
The conductor's flapping
like a pigeon now,
fluttering above
a spiked windowsill,
looking for tonic, for the home
hidden in that chord
John Williams stole from Holst
who stole it from Bach
who stole it from God
who stole it from himself.
What else can an orchestra do
but play? Then hold the final note —
tenuto, sostenuto — sustained
as if it were the world's only music,
held and held like this applause
for the old man,
the mirrors of our hands
banging together and breaking.

ANOTHER ANGEL OF THE CROSS

So again we are praying for rain,
our wrists in the handcuffs of prayer,
our minds full of thunderheads —

or trying to be. But instead of God
or prayer, I'm thinking ironically of sun,
and what my dog thinks about sun,

and then about that semi trailer
merging last week across the center line
toward the red pinwheel of my car.

I was singing the high,
light notes of a Mozart opera —
Cosi Fan Tutti, the end of Act I —

with its dangerous jumble,
that almost chaos of voice on voice.
And it looked like catastrophe —

my thoughts free-falling
into my stomach, into my testicles
where all those homunculi

Aquinas believed we harbor
now would never be born. Then
what I was praying for happened:

clouds, drizzle, rain, the truck
unmerging — demi- and semi-merging,
the homunculi and me all safe.

1939 E6   anderer Engel vom Kreuz

PLATE 21

I thought then God was
a low-flying plane, waggling
his wings hello, or roger, or ahoy.

But keep your eyes on the road:
We're praying for rain out here
at our little crossroads on the plains,

where nothing is secret, and dust
plumes behind every traveler
for miles, and the grid

is terrible in its meetings.
But I'm thinking instead
hello. Avast. Is that you, Roger?

Zweifelnder Engel
1940 F1

PLATE 22

DOUBTING ANGEL

And if I cried out
who would hear me?
(Prayer is just
a thickening of the air.)

And if I listened
what would I hear?
The music of a dog
dragging his chain.

Raising my hand
in the air as blessing
only requires
that I believe in air.

And whatever blessing
I gave would only be
the world's usual stutter,
the space between notes,

the silence already
tied in my hair.

1939 W.U. 5   im Vorzimmer der Engelschaft

PLATE 73

IN THE WAITING ROOM OF ANGELHOOD

Here my dreams are shifted slightly; my arms are always in the air when I wake up. I dream of singing, but of course my throat has other business. Mostly my body is completely on its own. Somewhere, in a hollow I used to have, is a little scar of pines and unstable grass. I miss the crisis of sparrows and the slump of water in useless pools. Oh God, who once was behind the door, this is a terrible room to wake in as if it were everywhere.

I used to have dreams I was a peasant with a monkey I could sing to. The songs were impromptu, the kind you find stupidly in the air. "Oh don't tell the monkey," I sang once, "oh don't tell the monkey, oh don't tell the monkey, that you are going away." Paul McCartney sorts of things. These were the ways my dreams really worked.

Usually it wasn't clear just who I was or where. But once I was a painter with a monkey. We would load a big canvas onto a wheelbarrow and wobble down the lane to the marsh where I painted the yellow grass and purplish water. The monkey handed me brushes I didn't need. I dreamed this, night after night, until the painting was finished, but by then it was of pines and the monkey had a blue shirt on and stole from me.

1939 YY 19   Mehr Vogel

PLATE 74

MORE BIRD

When we arrived
we couldn't speak the language.
All the new songs clogged our throats.
And so, like immigrants,
we caucused and flocked to ourselves:
Chuck-will's-widow, Whip-poor-will,
Egret growling "rarr" and "hraa."
"Jay," screamed the Jay.
The Grebe clanged.
The Black-throated Blue Warbler crooned,
"Please, please squeeze me."
It was more jeer than glee,
more attitude than prayer:
we were a smug Babel.

And then we exchanged
our wings for citizenship,
for hats to throw in the air
on the anniversary of our hats' arrival.
And then we were taken to the tenements.
There the Myna learned,
the Yellow-headed Parrot learned,
the egotist Jay, the Magpie, Macaw
all learned to flatter God
with the sound of his own voice.

The rest of us gathered on stoops and wires
remembering the old country and its plangent songs:
"Sweet Sweet Canada Canada Canada,"
sang the White-throated Sparrow.
"Sweet, sweeter than sweet," sang the Yellow Warbler.
"Pity," sang the Phalarope.

"Sit," said the Guillemot.
"Weep," sang the Bridled Tern.
The mute swan threw its hat in the air —
more bird, more bird than angel.

ANGEL OVERFLOWING

Christmas 1939, painted for Rolf and Käthi Bürgi

December. Our breath
hovers in the air
like shapes, messengers —

the way Christ was one
of the shapes
of the breath of God.

Most of the time we cannot say
what we mean
so we send effigies —

the word "levee" instead
of the levee itself,
a postcard of the flood

but not the real water.
So instead
of heaven, I've sent

this picture of heaven —
a paradise
so small we will need

to bow our heads hard —
harder
even than here —

just to stay in the picture.
Instead of me,
I've sent a line

gloriously out of hand,
a body
too small for its colors.

1939 NN 16   Engel, übervoll

PLATE 25

PLATE 26

ANGELUS DUBIOSUS

1.

God is outside inventing birds, but is arguing with himself over
    the shapes of their heads
Paul Klee has lapsed into Latin
As in to lapse into bad habits, lapse into heresy, lapse into reverie
Yesterday I found twelve lottery tickets in the long grass behind
    the potting shed
The moons of Uranus are named for Shakespearean heroines:
    Desdemona, Portia, Juliet, Umbriel
One can suck one's fingers over why:
    Rosalind, Cressida, Belinda, Miranda
    Titania, Cordelia, Ophelia, Bianca
Miranda's surface, apparently, is fractured as if early on she
    had been broken into shards and pieced back together
As in her membership lapsed after the first year, years have
    lapsed (or elapsed) since
If this were a democracy the birds would have a say

2.

"Angelus Dubiosus" is Latin, sort of
Reassembled
In 1604 Kepler invents the word "focus"
As in Latin for "fire," "hearth"
So that all planets had elliptical orbits with the sun at one
    of the foci
As in a lapse in judgment, a lapse into barbarism, from the pure
    Latin *lapsis*, a lapse of time, sin
Angelus-ay, Ubiosis-day
I've been up all night reading about this
Herschel discovers Uranus in 1781
The importance was to establish a standard
"Uranus" is Greek for "heavenly," a personification of the sky
Klee has applied for Swiss citizenship that will come a week
    after his death
God is outside inventing masks because birds turned out so ugly
It's 1933 and Lily Klee has been telling him for a year there
    is nothing left to do
Meaning in Germany, meaning the Bauhaus is over, the Academy
    gone
Meaning the noble Swiss don't want him any more than the Nazis:
    "It would be an insult against the true art, a deterioration
    of good taste, and of the healthy ideas of the population,"
    they said in German they said in French they said in Italian
Meaning the first Degenerate Art show has opened in Karlsruhe
Question: "Which of these three drawings is the work of ... an
    inmate of a lunatic asylum? You will be surprised"
Aphrodite was born in the sea foam of Uranus' genitals after his
    wife and children cut them off and threw them in the ocean
This is before democracy
Answer: "The one on the right above!"

3.

Umbriel?

The SS has abducted Klee's letters to his wife, the ones that
prove everything

Kepler, who had no idea of gravity, believed the solar system was
held together by the sun's virtue

The ticket numbers were 286, 287, 288, 289, etc

Next he will have to prove he is not a Galician Jew

Except for Umbriel. Who is a gnome in "The Rape of the Lock"

Except for Belinda who is a ditz in "The Rape of the Lock"

Except for Oberon, except for Puck

As if we've run out of heroines

Someone's gotten sloppy

The masks don't fit the birds

Most of the angels are pinheads

Donner, Blitzen, etc

From the Latin *virtus* meaning manliness, goodness, excellence,
etc

Trustworthy, Loyal, Helpful, Friendly, etc

Prospero: To th' most of men this is a Caliban, and they to him
are angels

Miranda: Good wombs have borne bad sons

Prospero: Shake it off. Come on

4.

God is outside inventing actors to wear the masks

Because Kepler eliminated the epicycles and deferents that made
    each planet special

The erect phallus and its uses, etc

Degenerate Art included: "Collapse of sensitivity to form and
    color," "draft-dodging," "moral program of Bolshevism,"
    "racial degeneration," "mental degeneration," "Jewish
    art," "sheer insanity," etc

Because in 1837 astronomers calculated "a disturbing influence"
    present in the solar system which led to the discovery of
    Neptune

But don't get me started on Neptune

Miranda, the guidebook says, "has some of the most dramatic
    scenery in the solar system"

Priapus, Hermaphroditus, Eros, Anteros are the children of
    Aphrodite

Which would explain a lot

Love and love's opposite shore

None of the tickets were winners

God is outside inventing the theater as we know it, for all the
    good it will do him

Think of the years Ptolemy and Copernicus loved the somersaults
    of the planets, their squirrel-like tumbling, their intricate,
    giggly math

Because beauty is the child of violence

Because Paul Klee is outside painting ugly angels, poor angels,
    groping angels, etc

Militant angels, angels of death, overfilled, listening, forgetful,
    alert angels

Angels still ugly, in crisis, in pairs, in threes, in kindergarten,
    in boats
Because faith is the twin of doubt
Because doubting is the meditation of the world
Because we are all on steep paths, on fire, full of hope
Because we are all angels kneeling, drinking, unfinished and
    dubious, wavering in the glare between worlds

Engel voller Hoffnung 1939 VII/12

PLATE 27

HOPEFUL ANGEL

It's only morning,
but already
I've used up my legs.

And already I've traded
stones for sight
my body for distance.

This is how I travel now:
mistaking myself
for something farther on.

Everything is immanent.
Hope is a cup
spilled, then righted

expecting to be filled again.
I've traded
my throat for a voice,

the road for sky,
the object
of prayer for prayer itself —

which is hope's alphabet,
which is pilgrims
groping their way, which

is H traded for
the lesser I,
but also for the promise

of J and its falling
stroke, then
its barnstorming rise,

its face and about-face,
its half cup,
its one wing in the air.

NOTES

"Last Earthly Step"
The opening lines are quotes and adaptations of Klee's theories of balance from *The Thinking Eye*. Lines 25 and 26, referring to history and progress, are a reworking of Walter Benjamin's discussion of Klee's "Angelus Novus," an angel from the 1920s, in Benjamin's "Theses on the philosophy of history."

"Angel Applicant"
Line 9 refers to Cezanne's painting "The House of the Hanged Man" ("La Maison du Pendu a Auvers").

"Angelus Militans"
The descriptions of the arrow, circle and spiral are adapted from Klee's *Pedagogical Sketchbook*. The arrow for Klee was a symbol of both limitation and hope. Gravity always defeats the arrow, but Klee exhorted his students to "be winged arrows, aiming at fulfillment and goal, even though you will tire without having reached the mark."

"Angel Still Groping"
Lines 5 and 48 are adapted from Vallejo's *Trilce* "XLV"; line 12 is a rough description of Leonardo's "Lady with an Ermine."

"Ugly Angel"
The penultimate line owes something (although ironically) to Rilke's "The First Elegy" in *Duino Elegies* where he identifies every angel as "terrifying." Klee and Rilke met in 1915 and were apparently on friendly terms until Rilke's death in 1926.

"Osaña"
Osanna Andreasi was a fifteenth century saint from Mantua. She apparently became ecstatic when she spoke of God and bore the marks of the stigmata. She is the patron saint of school girls; one of her symbols is a broken heart with a cross and lily emerging from it. There is no proof other than the spelling of the title that Klee had her in mind when he drew this angel.

"Doubting Angel"
The first line is an adaptation of the first line of Rilke's "The First Elegy"; the last line is a paraphrase of lines from Rafael Alberti's third of three poems entitled "The Good Angel" from *Concerning the Angels*.

"Angel Overflowing"
Christmas 1939 was Klee's last before he died. The painting was his gift of that year to Rolf and Käthi Bürgi, his friends and patrons. Rolf Bürgi was the son of Hanni Bürgi, one of the first great collectors of Klee's work, and he helped arrange Paul and Lily Klee's difficult move from Germany to Switzerland in 1933 when Klee was being harassed by the German police.